S0-AXO-619

FIRESIDE

DANTE'S
Infernal Guide to
Your School

BY FRANK BEHRENS

A Fireside Book
Published by Simon and Schuster
New York

Copyright © 1971 by Frank Behrens
All rights reserved
including the right of reproduction
in whole or in part in any form
A Fireside Book
Published by Simon and Schuster
A Division of Gulf & Western Corporation
Simon & Schuster Building
Rockefeller Center
1230 Avenue of the Americas
New York, New York 10020

ISBN 0-671-20975-2
Library of Congress Catalog Card Number 75-154091
Designed by Helen Barrow
Manufactured in the United States of America

8   9   10   11   12   13   14   15   16   17

THIS VOLUME IS DEDICATED TO

...my wife Shirley who did all the cleaning
the day I put the book together

...my daughter and son Susan and Richard
who tore off and handed me the pieces of tape
I used to attach the plates to the page

...all my wonderful students and associates
past and present who make me feel a little contrite
about comparing schools to the Inferno

...all the other less wonderful students and associates
who convince me that I have done
the right thing after all

...to Dante
whose wonderful work
I may some day actually read

AND MOST ESPECIALLY TO

...Gustave Doré
without whose genius I would have had to draw
all these pictures myself.

DANTE'S
Infernal Guide to Your School

Your graduation from college is only the first step
in your career as a teacher.

As a new teacher, you will feel a little lost
and out of place for the first few days.

Get acquainted with teachers who have been
in the school for a long time.
They can give you many helpful hints.

Much can be learned from the monthly faculty conferences.

Most schools set aside a lounge for the teachers to relax
in between assigned periods.

The custodian's office is usually located
in or near the basement.

He is there to be called upon
should your room be a bit too warm...

…or a bit too cool.

You will always find the principal ready to back you up when things get out of hand.

Overcrowded classrooms are a major problem.

If the room has not been left sufficiently clean,
you may have a little housekeeping to do
before the children arrive.

The most professional teacher is the one
who runs the quietest and most orderly class.

Make an attempt to learn the names of all your students during the first week.

Once seats are assigned, the children are not to change them for any reason without your permission.

Small children should not be allowed
to go to the bathroom unattended.

With the principal's permission,
small pets may be kept in the classroom.

Asking permission to get a drink of water is often a subterfuge for planned conviviality in the halls.

Any child with an injury, no matter how minor,
must be referred to the school nurse immediately.

Remember you yourself are not permitted to administer first aid of any sort.

But healthy outdoor sports are to be encouraged,
so do not allow minor injuries
or inclement weather to upset the schedule.

Twice a year you will be required to conduct a lesson
with a supervisor in the room.
Act as if he were not there and carry on as usual.

In schools where the children do not go home for lunch, discipline is sometimes required in the outside yard.

A student caught smoking on school grounds
must be reported at once.

Proper dress for Assemblies is still stressed in many schools.

To help you with these problems, you would do well
to appoint a boy large for his age as Monitor.

At times a group of children may decide to see
how far they can tempt you to lose your temper…

…but as a professional,
you will maintain control of the situation.

With a really bad discipline case, keep the child
under control and send for help.

A frequent problem is the child who is rejected by his peers.

One solution is to give him a special task to perform
in a position of some small authority
over those who formerly rejected him.

Give the children the feeling that you are available
at any time to help them with such problems.

Learn to spot
any child who should be placed in a special class.

Girls will tend to have more emotional problems
than will boys.

At times your job is made easier
when children themselves
point out a friend who has a problem.

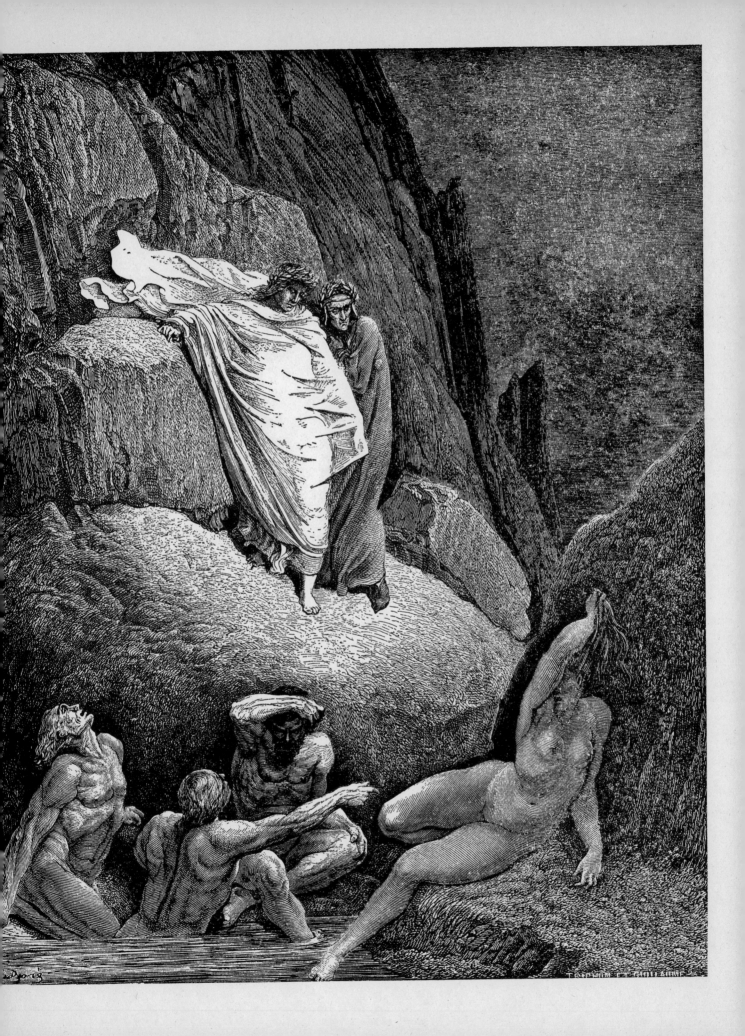

Many children form friendships which are inviolate.

Two or three times a year,
you will have the opportunity to see parents.

Some will tell you how they raised
and continue to train their children...

…while some will praise you
for the fine job you are doing
and leave the entire situation in your hands.
But be prepared to encounter some slight hostility
from some from time to time.

Above all, do not let a parent upset you,
as some may try to do.

Your most rewarding moment comes when a student thanks you for all you have done.

Every day at three o'clock you will leave the school
confident in the knowledge
that you have done a good day's work.

ABOUT THE AUTHOR

FRANKLIN ALLEN BEHRENS, *son of Mr. and Mrs. Behrens, was brought up in the Bronx, where he seldom wandered farther east than the Grand Concourse or farther west than Jerome Avenue, all this between 167th and 171st streets.*

After doing something not unlike adequately at the Bronx High School of Science, he went on to become an English major at the (then) City College of New York, where he became editor of the humor magazine Mercury *just in time to be nearly suspended for an offensive cartoon printed just before he became editor. From there he went to Lehigh University to teach English on an assistantship and to marry a girl named Shirley from Jackson Heights, Queens. They have two children, Susan and Richard.*

In recent years he has been teaching English, mathematics and science in New York City and editing a PTA bulletin.